Candle Making Explained

Candle Making for Beginners

The Art of Candle Making, Supplies, Ingredients, Types of Candles, Basic Candle Making Techniques, Marketing and More!

By Cynthia Cherry

Foreword

Candles have been the main source of artificial light for many centuries (around 5,000 years) until the electric light was invented around the 1900s. It has been an important component in human history as it's not just used at home or for household purposes but it's also utilized in events, travel, religious rituals, traditions, and various occasions such as holidays, birthdays, and other celebrations. Needless to say, no matter how subtle the candles' importance is, any event wouldn't be complete without it. Candles are simple yet very elegant and essential.

Candles are also one of the earliest inventions of humans after discovering fire! It simply uses wax in order to fuel and hold the light that it produces. When the wick of a candle is lighted up, the heat from it then burns the wax through a capillary action. Simple science isn't it? Our ancestors thought of that, and it blazed the trail for many things thereafter. The candles made humans conquer the night for thousands of years and it brought sustainable light everywhere they go!

Back then, the art of candle making were originally made out of beeswax which were produced from the honey combs of bees. Today, candle - makers use a candlewax and other types of wax in order to produce decorative and long – lasting candles that can be used for various purposes.

This guide book will teach you all the basics when it comes to the art of candle making. You'll also get to learn the brief history of how candles are used, the supplies and ingredients needed, the basic process of how to create one, and also the different types of candles which you can use for various occasions. You'll see that the possibilities are limitless when it comes to designing your own candles or the so – called Do – It – Yourself We'll also give you some tips on how you can market and raise funds for your candlemaking craft business should you choose to embark on this endeavor.

Table of Contents

Introduction to the Art of Candle Making

During the time of the Egyptians and early Romans, our ancestors made candles out of tallows which can be extracted from animals like sheep and cattle. These candles didn't burn as much, and according to historians the scent it produced stinks. The first one to create a candle quite similar to what we now have today was the people who lived during the Roman Empire. They've found a solution to make the tallows more efficient and less smelly by melting it and liquefying it. After doing that they will then pour it over fibers of cotton, hemp, or flax which are also used as a wick. It worked much better than the early versions, and from then on candles became a major component in religious ceremonies, at home, and also used during travel. This chapter will give you a brief history of how candles were used throughout the centuries, how it was used and developed in different countries/ culture, and how it stood the test of time and even became an art.

The Arts and Craft of Candle Making Throughout History

Candles originally started out as an artificial source of light since the dawn of mankind. The art of creating a candle have been developed in different countries, and is now being used today for various occasions, celebrations, religious/ ritual – related ceremonies, and even as part of home decorations.

According to historians, early Egyptians were one of the first civilizations to use candles and developed it; aside from candles, they are also known as the inventors of torches or anciently known as "rush lights." What ancient Egyptians did to create candles/torches is to use the animal fats, and soak it in the core of reeds. However, since the candles/ torches they made actually have no wick, it weren't considered as a real candle until the year 3000 B.C. This was the time when early Egyptians discovered that they can create a candle out of beeswax. Historians also accredits the ancient Egyptians of being one of the first people to create candle holders (which was made out of clay) because they've found such that dates back to around 400 B.C.

On the other side of the globe, around 221 B.C, ancient Chinese have also created candles that are made out of the animal fats but this time from a whale. They've eventually found a way to create one that's also made out of wax from seeds, and insects. They wrap this wax into a paper so that it can be burned.

During the time of ancient Indians, the art of candle making involved the boiling of the fruits from the cinnamon tree. They learned how to extract wax from it, and use it as temple candles. On the other hand, indigenous people who lived in the Pacific Northwest at the time of 1st century A.D., were able to create a lighting source by using the oil of the eulachon, which is also known as "candlefish." They simply stick the dried fish on a fork and light it up.

The early Romans during the time of the Roman Empire were the only civilization that came close to the candles that we now have today according to historians. They are highly credited when it comes to developing the concept of a candle with a wick; making it easy to light up and last for a much longer period. However, as mentioned earlier, the Romans use tallows as the standard material for making candles. Tallow is an animal fat that's produced by cattle, cows, or sheep; this has become the main candle material in Europe as well. However, the tallow produces a lot of smoke, and unpleasant smell since it's made out of animal fats. Nevertheless, they still used it during prayer or other religious ceremonies but because of the bad smell, it was banned in many European cities. When candles made out of beeswax was eventually developed, it became the main source of candles and were used for royal and religious events since it doesn't produce any bad odor. By 1415, tallow candles were only used as a street light.

The process of creating candles out of beeswax is pretty much the same with how the early Romans made candles out of tallows but of course, unlike the latter, beeswax is easier and cleaner when burned, and it also doesn't produce too much smoke – not to mention the pleasant odor. The only problem at the time is that beeswax is very limited and expensive which is why only the upper class and religious clergies can afford candle lights inside their homes/church. Tallow candles are still the most common household light source for the majority of Europeans.

Around the 13th century, the art of candle making became a craft in countries like Great Britain and France, and it also became a source of income for those who have time to do it because they found a way to use excess kitchen fats to create candles and sell it for a cheaper price.

Around the 15th century, the art of molding candles began in France. A new process/ candle technique was developed by simply pouring the wax over hollow and open – ended cylinders. They've put a cap that fits the cylinders so that the candle can be covered and placed a small hole for the wicks to be lighted. The wax was left to cool, and the wires holding the wick can eventually be taken off. During those times, candle makers spent about 8 to 10 days before they can create candles made out of wax and placed in a container.

When the art of candle making became quite popular, American's further improved the craft when they discovered how to extract the wax of bayberries and berry shrubs to give it a nice sweet smell, and color. It didn't really catch up at first and only a few people are doing this technique as the process is quite tedious since it will involve extracting bayberries. During that time 15 pounds of these berries can only produce about 1 pound of wax which is in the long run time consuming for candle makers.

Around the 18th century, when the whaling industry was booming, people found a way to use the wax obtained from the whale's sperm oil called Spermaceti to create candles. It was one of the first major changes in the art of candle - making as it provided a replacement to tallows, beeswax, and even bayberry wax. It's quite similar to beeswax because it's burns clean and pure, and also doesn't produce foul odor or smoky flames. In fact, it even produces brighter flame; aside from that, it's much harder when the wax has cooled compared to beeswax and tallow wax making it last longer even if it's placed under the sun. According to historians, the first standard candles came from the Spermaceti wax.

The 19th century was the defining moment for the candle making industry because this is the time when machines were utilized to develop batches of candles, making it easier, faster, and much more affordable to the public. Joseph Morgan was one of the inventors who developed a machine that can easily produce 1,500 molded candles per hour. It was also during this time that chemists, Michael Chevreul and Joseph Lussac, patented the stearin wax candles which are harder, easier to burn, and more durable. The candle making process experience drastic improvements when the stearin wax was invented because it improved the candles' quality; up to this day, candles made from stearin wax is one of the major components of candle – making in Europe.

It was also during the 19th century that wicks were improved. For years, wicks are only made out of twisted strands of cotton which burns poorly; fortunately, people discovered that using a braided wick or a wick that's tightly curled over is much better.

Around the 1850's, a substance called paraffin became commercially available. This is when inventor, James Young used and patented the substance to create inexpensive candles, that are of high quality, odorless, and also produces a bluish – white color. It also burns clearly, making the candle superior and much affordable.

Despite the drastic improvements of the candle making industry, it was soon threatened by the introduction of light in 1879, thanks to Thomas Edison. The candle – making industry began to decline, and was only used more as a decoration, and not as the main source of artificial light.

Today, thanks to the advances of technology and arts, the candle industry now offers a wide variety of candles produced from different kinds of waxes. You can now pick any color, size, shape, odor, design, and holders you like depending on where and how you're going to use it. Candles may not be the main source of light anymore unlike before but it's become a symbol of many celebrations, and important milestones in our lives. After all, birthdays wouldn't be complete without blowing a candle before you make a wish!

Chapter One: The Basics: Supplies and Ingredients

We've come a long way since the use of tallows and beeswax for candle making. Every century has found a way to improve the craft of candle making so that it'll be less smoky, easier and cleaner when burned, lasts longer, and also eliminate foul odor. Today, candles come in various shapes, sizes, designs, and fragrance. You can choose from a wide array of candles in the market today and even have an option to customize it. In this chapter we will discuss the different types of candles and purposes, the basic supplies you'll need to get you started, and explain to you the importance and use of each candle making ingredients. This will all come in handy later when we study about the different candle making techniques.

Types of Candles

There are various options of candles you can choose from nowadays; some candles are designed to freely standup, while some are intended to be a filler of a candle container or vessel. All of this can be classified under different candle types or categories.

Container Candles

These are a type of candles that's created from different kinds of wax and poured into a special container glass that is either tan or pottery. Container candles are the most commonly use candles at home because it is great for home décor, and gives off a very pleasant odor.

Votive or Molded Candles

Votive candles are the original type of free – standing candles that was first invented thousands of years ago. It usually comes in as a white molded candle that's also unscented. It's mainly used for religious purposes, and ceremonies. Nowadays, votive candles come in a various colors, and some even have fragrances. It's now designed to burn cleaner and lasts longer than the original version.

Pillar Candles

These are quite similar to votive candles since it's also free – standing. The only difference is that it has a more rigid structure and wider base. It's also available in various colors, fragrances and designs.

Taper Candles

This is a very slim candle that goes in an appropriate candle holder. It typically measures around 6 inches to 20 inches in length.

Tea – Light Candles

These kinds of candles are usually quite small and cylinder in shape that is placed in a polycarbonate container or aluminum candle holder.

Hurricane Candles

These are candles that contain some items embedded within the wax or added during the molding process. Sometimes candle makers add dried flowers, shells, and other designs depending on what the candle maker desire or if the customer wants it customized. It's also designed to burn down the middle area so that the outer shell can be illuminated.

Candle Making Supplies

Here are some of the basic things you'll need when creating candles. Some supplies may need to be added later on when we get to learn other candle type techniques but for now we'll just provide you a list of the things that are easily available to get you started:

- Wax (votive or mold; single pour)
- Coloring (powder dyes, color blocks, color chips, liquid dyes etc.)
- Additives (petrolatum, vybar etc.)
- Oil – based fragrance used for candle making
- Pouring pot
- Stove or other forms of heat source like hot plate
- Melting Heat Pot (presto pot, turkey roaster, hot water heater)
- Measuring spoons
- Measuring cups (preferably stainless steel)
- Stainless pitcher (this will be used to transfer the melted wax from the melting heat pot to the pouring pot)
- Containers (single – pour candles etc.)

- Wicks
- Molds
- Pan (13 x 9 size with ½ water)
- Candy thermometer
- Safety glasses and work clothes (optional)
- Floor mat
- Room temperature should be around 70 degrees

Candle Making Ingredients

In this section, you'll learn the different ingredients when making candles as well as its purpose and recommended measurements. Do take note that the recommendations and amount you use may vary so please just use it as a guide and adjust accordingly.

Wax

The first one on the list is wax, and the reason is because using or buying a quality wax can produce a quality candle. It doesn't matter how big or how fragrant your candle is if the wax isn't of good quality. There's a misconception among newbie candle makers that the more fragrant the candle is, the more durable or stronger it is. That's not the case because if you put a fragrance it will start filling up the pores of the wax, and once it's all filled up, there'll be no room for the fragrance oil anymore, and you'll end up wasting a lot of it; fragrance oils are quite expensive.

It's also important to note that you shouldn't buy more than 1.5 oz. of fragrance per pound of wax, otherwise the candles you'll make can end up becoming a fire hazard. It's best to just use pre – blended wax for candle making; this way you don't need to add any other additives because the wax manufacturer already did the job for you.

Whenever you're dealing with candle wax, make sure to read the instructions before using it. Temperature is very important in candle making as well especially during the wax stage; make sure to never heat up your wax to over 250 degrees Fahrenheit otherwise your wax will heat up and burn, and you'll have to start over again. You can't just pour fragrance oil to cover the burnt odor.

Fragrance

When it comes to using fragrance for your candles, it's best that you buy fragrance oils that are made for candle making. You should never ever use alcohol or some kind of perfume to add to your wax candle because it can become a fire hazard. You have many options when buying good fragrance oils for candle making purposes, some are quite expensive while some are more diluted than others.

If ever you decided to buy a concentrated type of fragrance oil, you should only apply 1 to 1.5 oz. per 1 pound of wax. Never go beyond 1.5 oz. otherwise you'll see it at the bottom of your pouring pot because the wax wouldn't be able to handle too much. There are companies out there that offers concentrated fragrance oils which can also be used for other types of candle wax (soy wax, gel wax etc.), and also bath products (Soaps etc.)

Coloring

There are various types of coloring that you can use when making candles, and each type has its own pros and cons. Take note of the following:

- **Color Blocks:** Color blocks are usually the most inexpensive yet quality means when coloring a candle. However, it could be quite difficult to use especially if you're a newbie because you won't always get accurate color results every time. Some people use a gram scale to ensure that the amount of color is just right but it can still fail. Some candle makers only use color blocks whenever they're making dark – colored candles only.

- **Liquid Dye:** Liquid dye can be a better solution for color accuracy but because of the chemical it contains, it can sometimes produce a bad odor. This is why some candle making experts don't use it when they're trying to create rich – colored candles. As a rule of thumb, some people opt not to use liquid dye if they need more than 10 drops of it per 4 pounds of wax because more than 10 drops per 4 pounds can make your candles produce a bad chemical smell.

- **Color Chips:** Color chips are usually expensive, and it's also not finely ground making it also quite difficult to use when it comes to achieving color accuracy. We do not recommend color chips but of course it's up to you whether you'll try it or not.

- **Crayons:** Crayons aren't an option if you want to produce a high – quality colored candle, and it's because crayons can clog the wick causing it to become a fire hazard. Never use this even if for some people it works out.

Candle Additives

Lots of candle makers use different kinds of candle additives mainly because it enhances the quality of the candles they produce. However, we do not recommend that you add a candle additive if you're going to use pre – blended wax. We will discuss below on what the properties of each additives contain so that you can better decide what's best to use in different kinds of candles/ wax you'll be making. Do keep in mind that the batches of candle wax will vary which is why you need to know how to adjust accordingly. See the following additives below:

- **Vybar Additive**

Vybaris is primarily used to enhance the "scent throw" of the candles. This additive can also make the candles more appealing, neat and opaque. It can also produce a marble – look at the top of the container candle. This additive also increases the melting point of the wax, and hardens the candle wax a little bit more.

If you plan on adding the Vybarto additive, it is best that you only use about ¼ to ½ teaspoon per 1 pound of wax, anything more than this measurement will make your wax overpower your fragrance oils.

There are two kinds of Vybar namely; Vybar 103 which is mostly is used for votive/molded candles, and the Vybar 260 which is commonly used for single pour wax candles.

- **UV Light Protector Additive**

The UV Light Protector is a very expensive kind of candle additive. If ever you would want to start selling your candle products to large suppliers/wholesalers, or simply start your own candle business, then it's best to not start using this unless of course the customer wants it.

The UV Light Protector additive can however improve the color quality of your candles, and also sustain its normal color even if it's placed under direct sunlight. Candles without UV Light Protector that's placed under direct sunlight can fade its color. But even if you add a UV light protector, it's still best to tell your clients to not let it burn under direct sunlight as it may become a fire hazard if not supervised. The colors that are usually fading when placed under the sun are burgundy, pink, blue, and violet.

If ever you opt to use a UV light protector, we recommend only using about ¼ teaspoon per 4 pounds of wax. If ever you find that the colors of the candles are still fading/ discoloration even after applying this additive then the problem may be because of the actual color of the fragrance oil you used.

- **Petrolatum Additive**

This additive comes in handy if your wax won't sting to the sides of your candle containers or your jars. You can add about ¼ cup per 4 pounds of wax. This additive will help increase the number of pores in your candle wax thereby allowing it to absorb more fragrance oils. However, the downside is that it can also cause a smoky flame when the candles are burned

- **Crisco Shortening** *Additive*

Crisco Shortening can help lessen the wet spots in the wax, increases melt pool, absorb more fragrance, and also decrease wasting fragrance oil on the bottom of your pouring pot. It's best that you use only 1 to 2 oz. of the Crisco Shortening additive.

Candle Wicks

When it comes to candle wicks, it somehow got a bad rep especially in the U.S. because the media reported to the public that candle wicks contain lead. The thing is that those wicks with lead content were mostly produced from other countries outside the U.S. The fact of the matter is that there isn't any wick manufacturer in the United States that produce lead – core wicks because most of them uses zinc to create candle wicks which is the best kind that one can use for candle making. Sometimes customers don't get that zinc is not a toxic content like lead.

This is why we recommend you use zinc – core based wicks because it's much better and burns nicely than using cotton wicks. It's also much safer than lead – based wicks. Zinc – core wicks usually burn cleaner compared to other kinds of candle wicks in the market, and it allows the entire candle wax to burn without any left overs making it worth your money or your customer's money. You'll see the difference if you have tried using cotton wicks or other core wicks.

We recommend that you use two pieces of zinc – core wicks that measures about 5 inches especially if you're going to use a 16 oz. jar though this is up to you because usually candle businesses only use 1 piece of wick.

You'll find our recommended measurements below. As you can see we've included the number and also the size of wicks that you can use when making candles. If you follow the measurements given, your candles will burn nicely, and slowly leaving no candle residues on the candle containers.

Candle Wick Chart

Candle Container	Wick Size	# of Candle Wicks
28 oz. apothecary jar	6" 44-28-18Z	2
16 oz. apothecary jar	5" 51-32-18Z	2
10 oz. Clear apothecary	2 1/2' 44-28-18Z	2
10 oz. Frosted apothecary	2 1/2" 44-28-18Z	2
5 oz. apothecary	5" 51-32-18Z	1
Flowerpot	2 1/2" 44-28-18Z	1
1.5 oz. Hexagon	1 3/4" 44-20-18Z	1
4 oz. Hexagon	2 1/2" 44-28-18Z	1
9 oz. Hexagon	6" 44-28-18Z	1
4 oz. Swivel Jar	2 1/2" 44-28-18Z	1
Country Jar (4 oz.)	2 1/2" 44-28-18Z	1
8 oz. Cylinder	6" 44-28-18Z	1
Votives (15 hour)	2 1/2" 44-28-18Z	1

Types of Candle Wicks	Recommendations
Zinc – Core Wicking	Commonly used in candle making; can be applied in different candle types
CD Flat Braided Coreless Wicking	Best use for soy or veggie candle wax

| HTP All Cotton Braided | Best use for soy or veggie candle wax |
| Hemp Core Wicking | An all - natural material; best use for soy or veggie candle wax |

Diameter or Size of the Candle	Recommendations
Tea Lights	1 2/4 inches Zinc Core Wick (44 – 20 – 18)
1 inch to 2 inches diameter of Votive and Candle Containers	2 ½ inches Zinc (44 – 28 – 18) 6 inches Zinc (44 – 28 – 18) 6 inches Zinc (44 – 24 – 18) 6 inches CD 5 2.5 inches HTP 31 6 inches Hemp (838)
2 inches to 3 inches diameter of Pillars and Candle Containers	6 inches Hemp (1400) 6 inches Zinc (51 – 32 – 18) 6 inches Zinc (44 – 28 – 18) 4 inches HTP 52 6 inches HTP 73 6 inches CD 7 6 inches CD 10
3 inches to 3.5 inches diameter of Pillars and	6 inches CD 12 6 inches Extra Large Zinc (62 –

Candle Containers	52 – 18)
	6 inches Hemp (60048)
	6 inches HTP 73
	6 inches HTP 83
With more than 3.5 inches diameter of Pillars and Candle Containers	6 inches Hemp (60048) 6 inches Extra Large Zinc (62 – 52 – 18) 6 inches HTP 104 for 4 inches diameter candles 6 inches HTP 1212 for 4.5 inches diameter candles CD 12 for 3.5 inches diameter candles; CD 14 for 4 inches diameter candles; CD 20 for 5 inches diameter candles; CD 22 for 5.5 inches diameter candles.

*Note: This wick measurement may not be applicable to every candle jar or candle type. Please just use this as a guide and adjust accordingly or best to ask the manufacturer on what measurements best suit the materials you bought from them.

Chapter Two: Preparing Your Working Area and Candle Equipment

Before we teach you the process of basic candle making and other candle making techniques in the next few chapters, it's important that you first and foremost prepare your working area. When it comes to candle making or any other activities for this matter, safety should always come first. You have to ensure that the candle wax and other flammable materials like fragrance oils or wicks are away from any heat source during your preparation to avoid any fire accidents. You need to also ensure that your floor area is covered, and every material you'll need is just close at hand. In this chapter, we'll give you a few reminders when it comes to candle making safety, what to do in cases of accidents, and also discuss with you the use of each material during the whole process.

Candle Etiquette

- Candles shouldn't be used as part of the table decoration if you are not planning to light it up during the meal. It's better to just put it away.

- Candle light should be blown away right after the people/guests leave the table to avoid any fire hazard instances.

- If you're going to use candles as part of your home décor, then make sure that they are not too lit up to avoid any accidents.

Candle Safety

When it comes to creating candles, you have to keep in mind that you're "playing with fire" or at least with a fire conductor material. You can reduce fire hazards and unforeseen accidents before and after your candle making process by following these precautions:

- Do not work near drapes or house curtains

- The base of the candle container should be non – flammable

- The base of the candle container should also hold the candle tightly so that it wouldn't fall over

- Never leave the candles or the wax burning in your work area. Supervise is a must.

- When you're melting the wax, make sure to do it in the pan that's set into a hot water and not melt it directly at the stove or direct heat.

- Do not use flammable trims or other flammable decorative materials in the candle such as dried flowers, pine cones, dried evergreen, ribbons, paper figurine, pine cones, cotton batting etc.

What to do During Accidents

- If the candle wax catches fire, immediately turn off the heat source, and cover the pot with the lid or use a fire blanket to smother the flames.

- Do not use water or other liquids to put out the fire as it can worsen the situation.

- If ever hot wax spills over your skin, don't wipe it off with a cloth, run it over cold water so that it would prevent the wax from solidifying. Use ointments to treat the burnt skin area just as you would treat a burn/scald.

Candle Equipment

Heat Sources

There are various types of heat sources that you can use when making hand – poured candles. Your heat source will affect the quality of your end products particularly when it comes to your fragranced wax. Check out the following equipment you can use below:

Turkey Roasters

Turkey roasters are quite common as a heat source if you're following a D-I-Y candles or Do –It – Yourself candle making. You can melt around 10 to 25 pounds of wax depending on how large the turkey roaster is. Usually it will cost around $100 to $200 or more depending on the brand or added functions. You can easily buy one at your local appliance shop or in Amazon. You may encounter sophisticated wax melters that can easily melt 100 pounds of wax but such equipment is much more expensive compare to buying turkey roasters.

If you choose to use turkey roasters, you need to make sure that there's around ¼ inches water under the roaster pan otherwise your candle wax wouldn't properly melt, and you'll also end up burning your turkey roaster so ensure that there's water underneath. That being said, you shouldn't add more water other than the measurement we mentioned because if you do, the water will just bubble out in your work area. This can also affect the quality of your candles because too much water can produce holes.

The turkey roasters should be set at 175, and it is best that you use a separate turkey roaster for single – pour candles, and votive candle wax otherwise your single – pour wax will require another pour. If the wax is slabbed, you can cool it using cold water but this can sometimes trap water in your wax so if that's the case, then just set your wax melter on a low, and allow the water to evaporate out of the candle wax. Ensure that the lid in your wax melter is sealed while you do it.

Stove or Hot Plate

Aside from turkey roasters, you can use another heat source like a stove or hot plate. Some candle makers only use turkey roaster for melting colorless, unscented candle wax with no additives. This is why you'll need another heat source in order to maintain your pouring temperature once you add color, fragrance, and additives in your candle wax.

What you can do is to take a 13 x 9 cake pan, and put around ½ inches of water on its bottom similar to how it's done with turkey roasters so that you can achieve a double boiler effect. You should make sure that the stove or hot place is only set in a low to medium heat settings though you can adjust accordingly depending on how easily your stove or hot plate can heat up.

It's recommended that you use a stove/ hot plate as a second heat provider so that you have your oven available to heat your candle containers later on. If your candle containers are quite cool, you'll need to warm them up a bit using your oven before you attempt in pouring the melted wax over it otherwise your wax will cool up, and it can produce jump lines in your candles.

Pouring Pots or Metal Coffee Cans

When it comes to pouring pots, some candle makers simply use coffee cans. This is a much cheaper option and it works just as well as actual pouring pots. If you do decide to use it, just make sure that you bend the lip of the can so that you can easily pour the melted wax out of it. You may need to use gloves or pot holders when doing this to avoid getting burned as the coffee cans may heat up once the melted wax is poured. We suggest that you have different types or separate pouring pots / coffee cans for each fragrance oils that you'll be using so that the scent and color accuracy wouldn't mix together or the quality wouldn't be jeopardized. You don't have to get a lot of pouring pots or coffee cans but just make sure you have as many as you can depending on the different colors/ fragrances you're planning to use.

You should also make sure that the bottom parts of the pouring pots are clean so that it would prevent hot water spilling over you. This is why you need to also make sure that you have safety glasses and other safety equipment so that you would not get harmed during the process especially if this is your first time doing this. As a side note, only use metal based coffee containers and not plastic coffee containers otherwise it will melt once you've poured in the hot wax. If you cannot find one, then just buy stainless pouring pots.

Candle Thermometer

When it comes to candle making, setting the right temperature is of utmost importance. You'll usually encounter many candle wax problems, and temperature is almost often the cause of it. As mentioned earlier, when it comes to doing single – pour wax, the temperature should be set at around 145 to 150 while the votive wax should be set at 160 to 165.

Votive Molds

Votive molds may cost you around $2 to $5 or more, and the great thing about it is that these votive molds are durable and can literally last for a long time. When using molds, make sure that it's set at room temperature before pouring the hot wax. As we've mentioned earlier, pouring hot wax into votive molds that are too cool can compromise the quality of your candles. Usually votive molds are stacked together when you buy them so just ensure that you use safety gloves when trying to get these votive molds separate because its edges are very sharp.

In order to keep your metal candle molds clean, you must rub it with a few drops of shortening, and placed it upside down in the oven for about 10 to 15 minutes at 150 degree temperature. Once you do, take it out and wipe it clean. Don't ever clean the metal votive molds with water.

The Right Room Temperature

Ensure that your room temperature is set at around 70 degrees. It's very important that when you're doing candle making, your candle wax should be in a favorable environment with the right temperature. Ensure that you also don't have drafts and there should be proper ventilation. If your work area is too cold, it can cause problems for your candle wax and end product.

Get Your Work Clothes On

This is optional but it is best that you have your work clothes on, preferably something that is simple and not flammable or doesn't have any sort of designs that can affect your candle making process. Even if you're very careful, sometimes you're going to get wax and color spilled into your clothes one way or another so it's better to get your old / work clothes on.

Floor Mats/ Cardboard/ Newspapers

All these materials will come in handy whenever you're working on your candles or melting your wax. It can also help prevent any accidents over spilled hot wax or fragrance oils, and it can also keep your floor tiles clean.

Measuring Cups and Measuring Spoons

Buying a stainless steel cups and spoons are highly recommended because it's much easier to measure fragrance oils when you use this kind of material instead of plastic otherwise the fragrance oil can easily dissolve your plastic measuring cups and spoons.

Chapter Three: Basic Candle Making Techniques

Are you now ready to create a candle? Don't worry because we will take it slow and we will first start with the basic candle making techniques. In this chapter you'll learn how to prepare a candle mold, melt the candle wax, the process of pouring the candle wax into the container, and also the steps on how you can finish the end product and also remove the mold. You'll also learn how to attach a candle wick into a wax, and how to pour a wax into a narrow neck container. This will all prepare you to other candle techniques we will show you in the next chapters.

Steps in Preparing the Mold

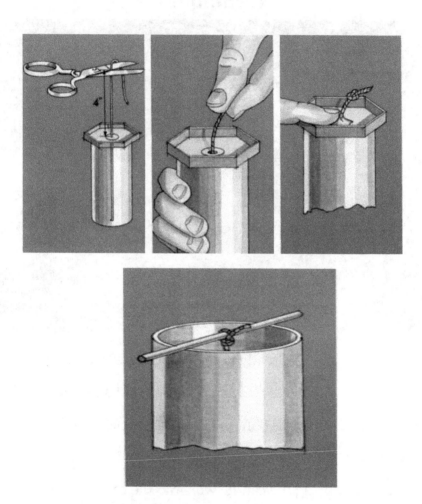

Step #1: Prepare all the materials you need. Keep the basic things we listed in the previous chapter at hand.

Step #2: Once you've done that, the first step in preparing the candle mold is to first make sure that the inside of it is clean.

Step #3: Cut the length of the candle wick and choose the size that will fit the mold or at least 4 centimeters longer than the length of the mold. After doing that, thread the candle wick through the hole in the bottom of the mold and tightly secure a knot.

Step #4: You or your customers of course will prefer the right length of candle wick over a short one, so make sure that you pull the knotted end of the wick at about ½ inches back from the mold before sealing it with the mold sealer.

Step #5: Place the wick holder across the top of the mold in order to secure it. You can use a cocktail stick to do that or other similar materials. Clip it and ensure that you centered the wick because if not, the candle itself will not evenly burn. You need to also tie a relatively loose wick to prevent it from bending.

Step #6: After placing the wick properly, you can now warm the mold and leave it in a warm area. Doing this will improve the candle once it's all finished.

Step #7: Fill the water: Bath it with relatively cool water.

Melting the Candle Wax

Step #1: Once your mold is good to go, you can now focus on melting your candle wax. Before you go and do this process, prepare your work area and materials as always. Do keep in mind the safety tips we gave you earlier, and never ever leave your wax unattended.

Step #2: Now that it's all taken care of, the first thing to do is to place some water at the bottom of your smaller sauce pan or pot then put a trivet into the bottom part of the larger one that contains the water.

Step #3: You can start placing a paraffin wax chips or other types of candle wax (about 1 pound) into the smaller saucepan. Once you've done that, you can now lower it into the larger sized saucepan and set it at a low heat source.

Step #4: Make sure to test the temperature once you see the wax beginning to melt. Again, never leave your melting wax unattended once it's already heated up. You should also constantly check on the water level at the bottom of your saucepan, and add a bit more if necessary.

Step #5: You can add stearin if you like. Should you choose to do so, you can add 3 table spoons per 1 pound of wax (for a colorless candle), and 2 table spoons per 1 pound of wax (for colored one).

Step #6: You can then add a color dye (just a little drop at a time), and test the color in a cup until you get the result you want or until the color is accurate.

Step #7: Remove the wax from the stove or other heat source once it reaches a temperature of 90 degrees Celsius

Steps in Pouring the Candle

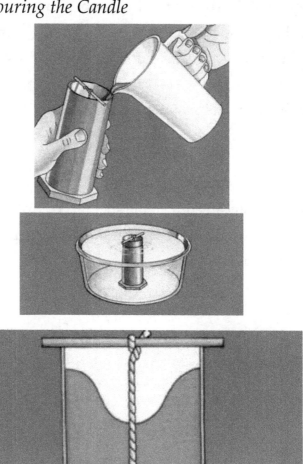

Step #1: Once you've already prepared the mold, and melted the wax, you can now start to pour your candle into the container. If you will want to add a fragrance, make sure to follow the instructions given on the bottle, and try not to waste it since fragrances are quite expensive.

Step #2: Move the wax pot or saucepan away from the heat source to your working area. You can use a Pyrex jug so that you can easily pour the melted wax into the container or mold.

Step #3: You can now pour the melted wax to the mold on its side. Make sure to tilt the mold a bit because this will prevent the air bubbles from forming which can spoil the candle once it's all cooled.

Step #4: Pour the candle wax or melted wax as much as the container will require

Step #5: If the melted wax is too warm, you can expect the finished product to form a pit mark spoiling at its surface due to the air bubbles of the steam. On the other hand, if it's too cool, the air bubble can also form on the surface spoiling your candle. This is why you need to ensure that the temperature of the melted wax is just right – not too hot or too cold.

Step #6: Place the candle in the water bath; make sure that the water level reaches the top of the mold or gets close to it.

How to Remove the Mold

Step #1: Remove the mold sealer, and use it for your other candle making projects. If you bought a quality mold sealer you can use it many times over.

Step #2: The next step after removing the mold sealer, you can now cut the now of the candle wick.

Step #3: Once you cut the candle wick, your candle can now slide quite easily from the mold if it's rigid. If the mold is made out of rubber, you can just peel it off.

Step #4: If your candle is obstinate, you can put it in the fridge for about 15 to 20 minutes. But if you're still unlucky, what you can do to persuade the candle from the mold is to pour hot water into it, so that it'll melt the wax that stuck to the sides of the mold in order for the candle to slip out. Of course if you do this, don't expect the candle will not have a smooth surface but at least you can melt it down.

Hot to Finish the Candle

Step #1: You can use a sharp knife to peel of the seam lines left by the mold

Step #2: Glazing your candle is optional but if you want to do it, you should glaze it before trimming the candle wick. You should dip the candle into a hot wax or water where no stearin additive has been included while you're holding the candle by its wick.

Step #3: Cut the wick to your desired length

Step #4: Level the candle's bottom through rubbing it on the inside of the empty and hot saucepan

Step #5: If you see that the candle's surface has your fingerprints, you can just rub it with nylon tights.

Step #6: You can use other materials to make molds such as jelly molds, yogurt, ice cube trays, cups, glasses, cream containers or small cute molds.

Candles Made Without Wicks

Should you choose to create candles out of improvised molds without a wick, you can add the wick by simply doing the following steps below:

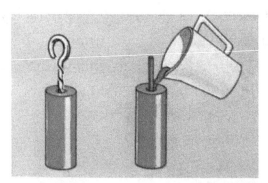

Step #1: You can insert the wick into the candle once you've removed the mold. Dip the wick into the warm wax, and pull it out.

Step #2: Create a hold in the candle's center using a heated skewer.

Step #3: Simply put the wick into the hole and then seal it by pouring a slightly hot wax around it.

Candles Made Using Narrow Neck Molds

You can also use narrow neck candle containers even if the bottom end is not that wide. However, you need to break the mold if you need to remove the candle. Some of examples of these molds include blown eggs, glass bottles, Christmas decorations and other similar materials. Do the following steps:

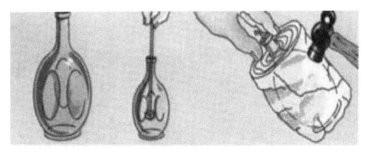

Step #1: You should tie a weight to the bottom of the candle wick before lowering it to the mold.

Step #2: Tie the candle wick to its wick holder.

Step #3: Create a candle and remove it from the mold by wrapping it in a towel, and then gently tap the mold with a hammer to break it and cause it to stop splintering. If you use a plastic container, you can trim the mold using a sharp knife.

Chapter Four: Other Candle Making Techniques Part One

In this chapter we'll teach you how to create one of the most common types of candles which is votive candles. Make sure to follow the steps and the see the photos as reference and additional instruction. You'll also learn steps on how to create other candle types like striped candles, diagonal striped candles, ice candles, mosaic candles, tinfoil candles, and free – form candle.

How to Make Votive Candles

Step #1: As usual, before you do anything, make sure to prepare all the materials you need such as the candle wax, the color dyes, fragrance oils, molds, additives etc.

Step #2: When it comes to creating motive candles, make sure to use the Vybar 103 additive because it is designed for motive candles. It's also important to note that the candle wax you'll use is specifically made for molded candles. You should not use petrolatum as an additive or a Crisco especially if you're trying to create a motive candle otherwise it would be difficult for you to get the cooled up candle wax out of the molds and you'd end up breaking it.

Step #3: The next step is to melt the wax, and prepare the wick (about ¼ inches), just like how we've mentioned it in the previous chapter. Once it's all done, you can now line up your candle molds, and pour the melted wax with the properly placed wick in it. Votive candles even if they are quite small in size are also a bit tricky, and you can definitely encounter some problems while making it. Compared with other candle types, you need to pour the wax twice because usually the votive wax sinks after the first one.

Step #4: For your first pour, what you need to do is to fill your votive candle molds; you should leave at least 1/16 inches of unfilled space in the candle mold. Otherwise, the second pour wouldn't be successful so don't fill it up completely the first time.

Step #5: For best results, we recommend that you save enough wax from your 1st pour so that the left over can be used for your 2nd pour; 4 pounds of candle wax can create around 32 candles. You can stop once you've done the 1st pour with 32 candles so that you can proceed to doing the 2nd pour.

Step #6: Votive candles can quickly cool up which is why you need to make sure that before it completely hardens, you've already straightened and place the candle wick in the center of the molds.

Step #7: Once it's all done, you can now allow your molded/votive candles to completely harden at room temperature for about two hours. After that, you can now do the second pour. Make sure to do it after 2 hours otherwise, your 2nd pour might sink. On the other hand, if you didn't do your 2nd pour and it exceeded 2 hours, the effect is that your votive candle will show marks of the 2nd pour.

Step #8: Place your pouring pot that contains your first pour left over in the stove, and set it at 160 to 165 temperatures. At this point, it is best not to add any fragrance oils otherwise it could cause the 2nd pour to have a slightly different shade than the 1st pour.

Step #9: After you've done the 1st and 2nd pour in all your votive molds, you need to wait for about an hour before you tilt the mold upside down in order to pop the votive – sized candles out. You're basically done at this point.

Step #10: If ever you need to create a slightly larger votive candle, you'll still need to follow the same steps but there are just a few differences. Take note of the following:

- You'll need to poke a few holes in your large votive candle after the 1st pour is set up in ½ inches to release any air pockets

- Larger votive candles will most likely need several wax re – pours depending on how large you want to make.

How to Make a Striped Candle

Here are the steps on how you can create a striped candle design.

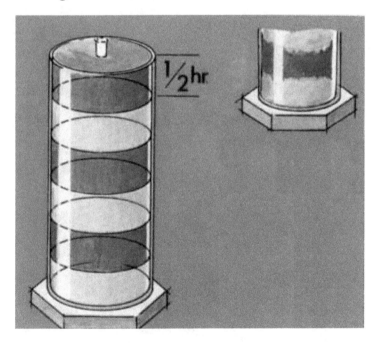

Step #1: First step is to prepped up your candle wax, your candle mold, and the color dyes you like in different containers. Never tilt the mold like what you do when pouring a single – colored candle.

Step #2: Next is to carefully pour the melted wax into the mold's bottom part. Let the layer set so that it'll be good for the color dye separation. If ever you want the colors to blend a bit then pour it while the first layer is still hot.

Step #3: Once it's all cooled up, remove it from the candle mold and place it in the box or candle container.

How to Make a Diagonal Stripe

Diagonal stripes just like the stripe candles are very appealing, and it's also not as hard to make as you think. Follow the steps below:

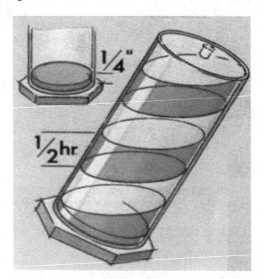

Step #1: Prepare the candle wax and the mold as well as the color dyes.

Step #2: Once the wax is already melted at the right temperature, you can now pour the 1st layer of wax to a depth of 6 millimeters or ¼ inches, and just let it set. Once the layer is set, tilt the mold and secure it.

Step #3: Begin pouring in the next layer. If ever you want to change the direction of the stripes, what you need to do is to move the angle of the mold when the 2nd layer is set.

Step #4: Once the pour reached the top of the mold, straighten it out before pouring the last layer.

Step #5: Let it completely harden, and remove the finished candle from the mold.

How to Make Ice Candles

You can get a certain effect once you've put ice cubes into the mold. When the candle is popped out of the mold it will usually have cavities. If you wish to achieve a perfect ice candles, then follow the steps below:

Step #1: The first thing you need to keep at hand is a core handle. You need to color dye the wax, and also cut the appropriate amount of candle wick.

Step #2: The next step is to pour the colored wax into a deep container, and then dip the candle wick into it. Once you've done that, you need to pull up the wick taut, and then just repeat the whole process until you built up a candle that measures about ½ inches or 12 millimeters in diameter.

Step #3: Make some ice cubes and then put it in the candle mold, then pour the melted wax over it. Just hold the mold over the sink so that you can remove the candle.

How to Make Mosaic Candles

Step #1: Prepare the mold, and the colored candle wax. You'll also need a baking try for this one.

Step #2: In order for you to create a mosaic chunk, pour the colored melted wax into an old baking tray. Once the wax is all cooled and set in the tray, you can now break it into chunks.

Step #3: Place the chunks into the prepared mold and ensure that the wick is also placed at the centered.

Step #4: You can start melting contrasting colored wax; just make sure to not add any stearin so that you can clearly see the contrasting colored chunks. You can use a pale shade of wax.

Step #5: Allow the colored wax to cool around 70 degrees Celsius. Make sure that the colored wax is not too hot when you pour it otherwise it can melt the wax chunks.

Step #6: You can slowly pour the wax in. As you pour it in you can see how the chunks bind together. Once it's all done, you can then remove the hardened candled from mold.

How to Make a Tinfoil Candles

Step #1: First thing to do is to cut some strips of tin foil and then crumple it. Once you've done that you can place it in the mold and then pour the melted wax in and add color dye.

Step #2: Don't add stearin otherwise you won't see the thin foil; the goal is to see the transparent effect. Once it's all done, you can then remove the hardened candled from mold.

Free Form Candles

How to Make Sand Candles

Step #1: You'll obviously need a sand to do this type of candle. Place clean and a bit damp sand in a small bucket, and then make any sand shape you like.

Step #2: Once you're satisfied with the shape, you can now pour the melted wax into the sand. You need to allow the wax to set in, and once it does you can now remove the candle from the mold.

Step #3: You need to create a hole in the sand candle using a hot skewer so that you can insert the wick. After doing that you can now fill the gap between the candle wax and the wick.

Candles Made In Heavy Duty Polythene Bags

Step #1: Push the bag into a glass jar, and then let the top of the bag hang up around it.

Step #2: Melt the candle wax and turn off your heat source once the thermometer registers 80 degrees Celsius. Let it cool until you see a scum form on its surface.

Step #3: Once you've done that, you should now slowly pour the melted wax into the polythene bag, and then allow it to cool.

Step #4: When the wax is still pliable, you should remove the bag from the jar and carefully slip a rubber band on the top. This way you can mold the bag with soft wax, and shape it up in any way you like.

Step #5: Put the bag into the cool water so that it can completely harden up. Once you've done that, you can now release the candle by simply removing the rubber band, and tear away the bag. Finish the candle by inserting the wick.

Chapter Five: Other Candle Making Techniques Part Two

When it comes to candle making, there's an almost unlimited options and candle types. You can even customize the candles to your customer's liking or whatever shape, texture, size, and color you'd like. This chapter will provide you with additional candle making techniques that can hopefully inspire you to come up with your own designs. Once you've mastered the basic candle making technique as shown in previous chapters, you can now move on and try creating frosted candles, ice cube candles, aluminum foil candles, stacked candles, floating candles, marbleized candles, glow candle, and candles made out of beeswax sheet.

How to Make Frosted Candles

Step #1: Prepare your materials and follow the basic candle procedure we've listed in the previous chapters. Basically, you can begin with any candle shape you like to start off the frosted candle process.

Step #2: Start melting your paraffin wax, soy wax or any candle wax type you like. You can also add any color dye you desire. .

Step #3: Let the melted wax cool up until the mixture starts to harden.

Step #4: Whip it to a froth using an egg beater or fork

Step #5: Apply it to the candle using a fork, or you can also turn the candle in the frosting until it's fully coated. You don't necessarily need to cover the entire candle because some bare spots and texture contrast add to the appeal or design of the finished product

How to Make Ice Cube Candles

Step #1: The first thing you need to do is to gather up some ice cubes, and then proceed to finely breaking it. Uneven sizes usually create different size holes so that's fine. A whole ice cube on the other hand usually creates quite a huge hold for the candle to support itself.

Step #2: Make sure that the wick is at the center of the candle mold. You can use a milk carton as it works best with this type of candle.

Step #3: The next step is to pack the ice cubes around the candle wick to as high as what you want your candle to be.

Step #4: Once you've done that you can now carefully pour the melted paraffin/soy wax into the mold. Don't forget to shake the mold a little as you pour the hot wax. Once the wax reaches the top of the ice cube, you can now set the mold down, and just leave it until you see the wax hardening; the ice cube will eventually melt.

Step #5: Drain out the water and remove it the finished candle from the mold.

How to Make Aluminum Foil Candles

Step #1: The first step is to create a bunch of balls into different sizes using a crumpled aluminum foil.

Step #2: The next step is to place the candle wick in the mold, and prepare your melted wax.

Step #3: Once you've done that you can now carefully pour the melted paraffin/soy wax into the mold. Don't forget to shake the mold a little as you pour the hot wax.

Step #4: Fill the mold with the crumpled aluminum foil, just as how you did it with the ice cubes in an ice cube candles. Once the wax reaches the crumpled aluminum foil, you can now set the mold down, and just leave it until you see the wax hardening.

Step #5: Do not remove the crumpled aluminum foil balls from the finished product.

How to Make Stacked Candles

Step #1: You can make molded candles with no wicks attached using cookie cutters, tart shells, jelly molds or other similar shaping materials as your candle molds. Just ensure that the top of the shaping materials is very flat.

Step #2: You can choose different mold colors, and be sure that the colors are appealing to each other.

Step #3: Remove the candle from the molds, and then stack it on top of each other, either upside down or the right side up.

Step #4: Once you've stacked them up on whatever side you chose, the next step is to stick them together using the melted paraffin wax. Proceed on melting the candle wax and pour it inside the mold. Let it cool and harden after about an hour.

Step #5: You can add a candle wick by using a hot skewer. Simply poke the center of the candle stack and insert the wick. Pour in a bit of hot wax to seal it off. Let it set.

How to Make Floating Candles

Step #1: Choose a relatively small tart shell, jelly mold, cookie cutters and use them as candle molds. The molds should measure around 3 to 4 cm.

Step #2: If the mold has a bottom or top, make sure to lay it flat on the wax paper and pour a thin layer of melted wax, and just let it harden up. Once the bottom is all waxed up you can finish pouring in the melted wax. If ever there's a handle or hole on one side, you can cover it using a few layers of masking tape.

Step #3: Insert the candle wick once you see the candle starting to set.

Step #4: Once it's all done, you can now place the candle on the candle holder, and let it float on top of the water.

How to Make Marbleized Candle

Step #1: Put a thin candle wick in the center of a mold

Step #2: Melt about 2 bars of candle wax in a separate pouring pot. You can add any color dye to each of the bar.

Step #3: Pour the color into separate shallow pans, and let the wax harden.

Step #4: Break the cooled wax into pieces and then place it around the candle wick. Make sure to alternate the colors while you dump the pieces for added effect.

Step #5: Let it set and then remove it from the mold to get the finished product.

How to Make Glow Candle

Step #1: Follow the procedures we've listed in the Frosted Candle section.

Step #2: Blow up a balloon. Make sure that the balloon is thick and of quality because regular balloons will easily break.

Step #3: Freeze up the entire balloon and leave around 2 inches in diameter of unfrosted space. The frosting should be quite thick. You can let some of the air out when the frosting gets hard. Once it does, remove it from the candle.

Step #4: Soften the wax on the end that's opposite to the hole, and then press down the base of it so that the candle gets flat.

Step #5: Drip a little of the candle wax inside the bottom of the candle, and then stand a thin candle in an upright position. When the thin candle is lit, you'll see that the outside doesn't melt too much but it produces a glow.

How to Make Beeswax Sheet Candles

There are 2 ways of creating candles out of beeswax sheets. Check out the following procedures below as well as the materials you'll need:

Method #1: Rolled Beeswax Candle

Materials:

- 16″ x 8″ size of beeswax sheets
- Candle Wick
- Hair dyer

Instructions:

Step #1: If the beeswax you bought is rolled then carefully unroll it. If you find that the beeswax sheet is stiff, or it cracks as you roll it, you can warm and soften it up by setting the hair dryer on a low.

Step #2: You can lay a piece of candle wick on one of the short edges of the beeswax sheet.

Step #3: Once it's all done you can simply roll it up, and proceed on the basic candle making.

Method #2: Cookie Cutter Candles

Materials:

- 16″ x 8″ size of beeswax sheets
- Candle Wick
- Cookie cutter
- Hair dryer

Instructions:

Step #1: The first thing you need to do is to lay the beeswax sheets separately on your cutting board.

Step #2: You'll need a cookie cutter for this so that you can cut around 5 shapes from the beeswax shit (or more if you choose to create a thicker candle).

Step #3: Get the wick in between of the wax layers, make sure it is centered. Leave at least ½ inch at the top of the candle, and then proceed on pressing the wax shapes. If ever the wax and the wick didn't stick well enough you can warm it up with a hair dryer and the set it up on a low.

Note: To burn the candles, make sure to secure it on another piece of beeswax sheet or on a surface that's non – flammable.

Tips in Cleaning Up

Tip #1: As we've mentioned in previous chapters, you should protect your table or tile surface from candle or wax drips by covering it up with plenty of newspapers, cardboard, or other similar materials otherwise the drips can cool up and harden in your table or tiles which could be quite hard to remove.

Tip #2: The pouring pans, candle molds, turkey roasters, and other candle making materials should be thoroughly cleaned before and after use. You can also sterilize it when not in use.

Tip #3: To dissolve the final thin coating of wax that's quite commonly found on the kitchen utensils. You can clean it up by soaking paper towels with methyl hydrate. After you wiped off the wax coatings, make sure to wash the utensils with soap and warm water. Rinse it thoroughly to remove the methyl hydrate.

Tip #4: To remove wax from your clothes or tablecloth, you can easily scrape it off using a knife. Just be careful though so that you won't tear off your clothes or hurt yourself. You can wish to place the cloth in the fridge to harden up the wax as it could be much easier to break or scrape. For you to remove the remaining wax, you can also place the cloth in blotters and iron it up a bit. If a stain remained, you can use a spot treatment soap and wash it off.

Evaluation

- Does the candle measure up to safety standards?
- Are the candle trims non – flammable?
- Is the candle base non – flammable?
- Does the trim and base suit the overall design of the candle?
- Do the color combination, texture, and color quality of the end produce looks appealing along with the base and trims?
- Is the finished product clean, free from finger prints, smooth, free from air bubbles or any other marks of a second pour?
- Is the wick properly set in the center and is it straightened up?
- Is it placed in an attractive candle container that matches the type of candle?

- Is the wax made of high quality and is not something that can break easily?

Chapter Six: Troubleshooting and Business Operations

This chapter will teach you some things when it comes to troubleshooting your candles. This is particularly helpful for those who are newbies at this craft. Whether you are just creating candles for personal purposes or you're planning to turn this passion of yours into a business you'll surely encounter troubles and mishaps along the way, and that's alright because this is how you're going to learn and become expert at candle making. This chapter also includes some guidelines when it comes to running a successful candle making business. We've given tips on how you can train your employees so that you can all work together efficiently and ensure that your products are of great quality!

Troubleshooting

Problem	Possible Causes	Solutions/ Remedy
The candle is producing too much smoke once lit up	There's high oil content. The candle wick might be too large. The candle may have plenty of air pockets.	Lessen your amount of fragrance oil Trim the wick to a shorter length Pour the candles at a much warmer temperature
The candle doesn't give off more than enough scent or it's not that fragrant.	Perhaps the fragrance oil you're using is of low quality. You didn't use enough fragrance oil. You added too much vybar additive.	Try buying a much better quality of fragrance oil Make sure that you use around 1 oz. of fragrance per pound of wax Make sure that the vybar additive is only around ½

	You may have left your candle wax in the heat source for too long that caused the fragrance oil to diminish. The candle wax you are using may not be porous.	teaspoon per pound of wax You need to pour your candles right after you add your fragrance oil Try using a more porous wax
Fragrance oil seems to always settle down to the bottom of the candle	You may have used plenty of fragrance oil. The candle wax you are using may not be porous.	Make sure to only pour in 1 oz. of fragrance oil per pound of wax. If you observed that the oil is slicking on the bottom of the saucepan or pouring pots, then stop pouring in the melted candle wax before you get to the oil because if

		you don't do this you'll surely end up seeing the fragrance oil at the bottom of your finished product.
The second pour is not blending well with the first pour of the melted wax.	Perhaps your 2nd pour is poured in a much cooler temperature	Try to do your 2nd pour while your candle is still a bit warm. However, you need to be careful and not pour the second one too soon otherwise; it will just sink just like your 1st pour.
The candle wax is not evenly burning all the way down.	Your candle wax may be too hard due to a high melting point. Your candle wick might also have a shorter length.	You should consider using a lower melt point candle wax. You can also try using a larger or longer wick. Take note

		that zinc core wicks and CD wicks usually tend to burn hotter than other types of wick.
The wick is drowning out in the candle.	Your candle wick size might be too small for the size of your candle. Perhaps you poured your candle above the point where the container begins to change shape	You should try using a larger candle wick. Make sure that you pour your container candle to the point where the jar starts to change its shape. Otherwise, going above the point will make the melted wax drown the wicks out once it's lit.
Candle doesn't come out of the candle molds you used.	Perhaps it's because you poured the candle when it's too hot.	Try using a harder wax or use a mold releaser. Make sure to also pour your

	You may have also poured your re – pour on the fill line. Your candle wax might be too soft.	melted candles at a lower temperature and don't pour the 2nd pour above the line of the 1st pour. You can also try putting the candle in the fridge to help it pop out from the mold. Don't place it in the freezer because the candles will crack.
The candles tend to create "jump lines" (these are the lines in the candle that can be seen on the skin of the wax or even outside of the candle container).	You may have added much stearic acid. Your mold could also be too cold when you poured your candle.	Try to warm your candle molds a bit before pouring a much hotter temperature. Make sure to use just the right amount of additives.

| Candles formed small air bubbles that lead to small air pockets or holes. | There's probably some water in the wax when you were pouring it.

You may have poured your 2nd pour above the 1st pour fill line.

Your candles might have cooled up too quickly or you poured the candles at a colder temperature. | Make sure you never get water into your candle wax when you do your pours this is because water is wax's worst enemy.

Make sure to also pour your melted candles at a lower temperature and don't pour the 2nd pour above the line of the 1st pour. The air will get trapped and it wouldn't get released before the candle has already set in.

Try to warm your candle molds a bit before pouring a |

		much hotter temperature. You should also make sure that your work area's temperature isn't too cold.

How to Run Your Candle Making Business Efficiently

Let's say you or your partner decided that you really love creating candles, and you also have considered making a business out of it since you already know the whole candle process, you already know where to get the cost efficient supplies, you have developed your own system on how to do things, and you may have already built a network of repeat customers. Now the next step is to grow your business so that you can make it more sustainable which means that it will require you to hire employees to help you or your partner out. Once you get to this point, you need to simplify the process and you should come up with a more organized plan suited for your goals and your resources so that your candle making business will run efficiently.

If you hired employees that already have an idea or experience when it comes to making different kinds of candles, then the process would be a bit easier when it comes to training them. However, if they don't have any experience whatsoever, then it's a must that you put in the time to really train your employees well and take small steps at first so that they have the right foundation, work – ethic, and knowledge. Keep in mind that candle making is a craft that only a few people know so most likely you'll end up hiring people that are not experts at this craft, it will take time to build and develop this skill so don't forget to also take it easy on them. Make it a fun and educational activity so that your team will enjoy working with you and learning from you. If you establish good rapport with your employees early on, your business operation will run efficiently in the long – term.

You also need to explain to them the step by step process of candle making. Make sure to emphasize the importance of quality is better than quantity. You need to let your employees know who your customers are and what kind of quality they expect so that your employees know what kind of people are buying your products and how these customers are using the crafts they'll be making.

Here are some more tips for running a smooth candle making operation:

- Let your employees know how many candles they need to produce per hour so that your business don't go under the quota otherwise this will incur labor cost on your company.

- During training, show your employees how quickly and efficiently you can create candles so that they'll have a desire to replicate the same efforts.

- During training, you should also point out their mistakes if need be. You should of course do it through positive criticism. If you need to tell someone of the mistake that they made, do so by first telling them what they did right, before telling them the mistake they made. Start off with complements or positive statement before pointing out the negative. Do it politely but firmly so that they can remember not to do it again thereby improving their overall work/ result.

- Make sure that your employees have someone they can easily ask questions about the process if ever you're not around. If there isn't anyone like that, and your office is quite far from their work area, it's a good idea to place an intercom system so that they can easily ask anything from you just by pushing a button. This way, you're still connected with them even if you're on to something else, and they will also feel that you're an approachable boss.

- Communication between you and your employees is very important. Keep in mind that they're the ones who are going to make candles for you on a daily basis, which is why it's wise to make them think of their own ways on how to do their job more efficiently, ask them for suggestions, and listen to what they have to say. You can even offer some incentives if any of them will suggest a more efficient way on how to run things. This way you'll make them feel that they are valued; they will feel that they are part of the company and part of your success!

The next section will delve deeper on how you can train your employees and some tips on what you can do when it comes to setting up the work/ production area.

Training Manual

Before we guide you step by step, it's important to note that your candle wax is already turned on for at least two hours prior to your worker's training schedule, otherwise, they wouldn't be able to pour the melted wax for the first 2 hours that they are scheduled. Do take note also that this training manual should only serve as a guide so that you'll have an idea on how to manage your employees especially if they don't have any experience in candle making. This is also a good place to start if it's your first time training people or running a candle making company, just make the necessary adjustments and act accordingly.

The following tips are what you need to show your employees so that they'll have an idea what kind of work ethic you have, and how the overall process works.

Training Tip #1: Instruct and remind your employees to always clock in or log in on their specific work schedule so that they get to practice the habit of going to work on time. This is also a way for you to monitor them. You may want to give incentives to those people who never miss a day or those who always gets to work ahead of their schedule (early birds).

Training Tip #2: As mentioned earlier, make sure to turn on your heat source to a low – medium setting, and ensure that the larger pan or bottom pan has around ½ inches of water.

Training Tip #3: We recommend that you list all the materials you need and have a sort of work order sheet so that you won't miss out on anything, and you know exactly what needs to be done in order of priority. It's also helpful especially when it comes to deciding what kind of fragrances you'll need to pour in your candles and which candle containers needs to be filled etc.

Training Tip #4: Start preparing all the materials you need including the fragrance oils, pouring pots, color dyes etc. Place all the pouring pots or sauce pans that will fit in your heat source and set the remaining pouring pots for the next batch near the stove or heat source so that when the first batch is done, the next batch is all prepped – up and is also accessible to you/your employees. You see if you already have a system in place and you already prepared the things you'll need and do, you and your employees will get to save lots of time, and the work becomes easy and efficient in the long run!

Training Tip #5: Go back to your work order sheet or your checklist to make sure that you don't miss out anything, and see if the container that needs to be filled for the day is all done. Pull all the containers and prepare them on your work area.

Training Tip #6: You can use signs like an asterisk to see what specific fragrance oil or color dye needs to go to certain candle containers, it will also serve as a reminder to your employees on the things that is of top priority during their shift.

Training Tip #7: Fill the pouring pot up to the line that's scratched inside it. Don't forget to remind your employees to fill appropriately all the pouring pots that needs filling.

Training Tip #8: What you can do to ensure that the amount of fragrance oils, color dyes, and other additives is to write down including the name of the fragrance, exact color amounts that needs to be added in each pouring pot to avoid any mishaps.

Training Tip #9: Make sure that you employees have their own work order sheet so that they know what needs to be done during their shift and what needs to be carried upon on the next employee that will do their job. Make sure to also put fragrance labels on the side of the jars that your employees will be using. It's important that you / your employees label it properly for 2 reasons; the first one is that it'll help prevent your employees from forgetting what needs to be filled, and the specific fragrance that should be used for each container. Make sure to place the unused fragrances in appropriate places and also label them up so that it'll be easy to find and identify during production.

Training Tip #10: Instruct your employees to always start with one of the fragrance oils that have a priority sign based on the work order sheet. Remind them to never add fragrance oils to the pouring pots until everything is checked and is ready to go in order to avoid any wasted oils as fragrances are very expensive.

Training Tip #11: Make sure to show your team how to properly fill the entire candle molds/ containers as well as the sizes and number of candle wicks needed for each candle. Post your reminders and candle size guides/ charts on the wall for their reference.

Training Tip #12: Fill all the molds to the appropriate pouring line, and remind them to wait until the first pour is starting to settle on top of the mold. Make sure that they'll use the appropriate wick size for each candle type.

Training Tip #13: Once each step is done for each candle mold, make sure to place the pouring pot back to its alphabetical location on the shelf so that it can be easily accessed by the next employee. You can also let your employee mark the working sheet by putting a check mark including the finished container so that there wouldn't be any form of duplication or wrong finished products.

Training Tip #14: Make sure that before the candles are move, your employees should be able to see an obvious thick creamed film on top of it. Once they do, move the containers to the back of your working bench so that there'd be room for your next batch of candles.

Training Tip #15: Repeat all of the steps at least an hour before the scheduled training time so that you'll see if your employees can do it by themselves efficiently.

Training Tip #16: Once everything is set up, the next step is for you to check your employee's work at the end of the day. Check if the quota was made and if the end product is of good quality. Take note of the employees who made it so that you'll know what needs to be improved or who needs to be complimented etc.

Training Tip #17: Don't forget to also instruct them to put company labels on all your products. Once it's done, move all the products to the fulfillment or finishing area, and separate each candles according to their types so that it'll be ready to go and easy to identify come shipping time.

Training Tip #18: Once it's all placed properly in the finishing area, go back to the production area and check if all the pouring pots, fragrance oils, color dyes, additives, wax, wicks, and all candle making materials are placed on the right shelves and are cleaned up before you let your employees leave their work area.

Training Tip #19: After doing all of that, what you can do at least in the first few weeks is to let your employees fill up an "Improvement form." This is where they can suggest how to speed up the process, how to do things more efficiently and of course your comments so far on what they need to perhaps improved on and also positive affirmations about their work. This way, you and your employees can measure if the goals for the day are met and the things that they might need to work on.

Training Tip #20: Log out! Remind your employees to clock out after their shift, and if ever they did an overtime then make sure that you give them compliments/ incentives or thank them for their service.

Tips for the Second Shift

The second shift will carry on with the work done or unfinished by the first shift. Usually the second shift workers need to allot 1 ½ hours before they log out to ensure that they accomplish the extra end of the day duties.

Tip #1: The second shift workers will be the one primarily in charge of setting off all the heat sources and burners since they're the last one who's going to use it.

Tip #2: Remind them to also ensure that the benches or tables as well as the pouring pots and stoves are cleaned. Make them scrape off the wax if there's any.

Tip #3: Make sure that they don't forget to turn off the lights and close off the store if ever you wouldn't be around to do that. Assign a person to double – check everything before locking up the work area, and make him/her report to you after the last shift.

Suggested Work Area Layout

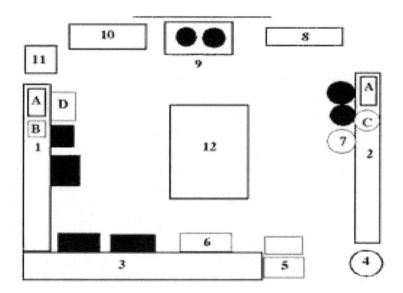

Chapter Seven: Tips in Establishing Your Candle Making Business

This chapter will focus on several important aspects when it comes to setting up a candle – making business, should you want to take your candle making skill to the next level. As what you've learned from the previous chapter, you'd most likely need to delegate tasks to your employees if you decide to make a business out of this craft, aside from doing that, you have to keep in mind that you're going to establish a business from the ground up which is why you need to plan about it from the conception of the candle ideas, to building a brand, and selling your products. We'll guide you on how to do that in this chapter.

Candle Design and Style

When it comes to starting a candle business, one of the first things you need to consider is what kind of candles would you want to produce, the different designs/ style you want to create, and perhaps which types of customer/ market is it intended to. If you're a beginner or a newbie when it comes to setting up your own candle making business, and you're just planning to start at the comfort of your home, you can begin by focusing on 1 or 2 types of candle styles. You don't need to start producing lots of designs at the onset assuming that you're only doing this by yourself. It's best that you start becoming an expert with at least one or two candles, and then move on from there. The most common types of candle design are container candles, mold/ votive candles, taper candles, and single – pour candles.

Choose the Type of Wax, Wick, Fragrance Oil, Color Dyes etc.

After deciding the kind of candle you want to produce for your business, we now go down to the supplies you'll need to create your finished product. You need to decide what type of wax you'll use. As mentioned in the first few chapters of this book, you can use the popular ones such as paraffin wax, bees wax, soy wax, and vegetable wax. After choosing the type of wax you'll use, the next step is to select the appropriate size of wick and the quality of wick that'll go into it. Review the first few chapters of this book as to the kinds of wax and wick is best suited for the type of candle you want to produce. It's also important that you know what kind of fragrance oil and candle additives to use in different candles. This is entirely up to you and the kind of design you want to make but just make sure it will complement the finished product, the amount you put in is enough, and the product itself (color dye/ fragrance oil etc.) is of good quality otherwise it'll ruin your finished product.

Master Your Candle Making Technique

Now that you have an idea on how your candles will look, the next step is to master your own candle making style or technique. This is very important because it will serve as the "bread and butter" of your business. You can have all the quality candle wax, wicks, fragrance oils, additives, supplies, skilled employees and even a great marketing/ business plan but if you aren't skilled enough to create basic candles, your business will never be successful and you won't have repeat customers. At the end of the day, it all boils down to your knowledge and experience, if you keep practicing and keep on improving yourself, you'll eventually find the right style/ technique that will work best for you and your skill level. Never stop learning from your mistakes, and continuously develop this craft so that you can become an expert at it. When you do, customers will surely see that your products are of great quality, and they will always want to buy from you. Mastering your craft will go a long way, and it's also something that you can pass on to your team. Developing a system is also important so that your employees adapt good work ethic, efficiency, and rapport.

Adapt a Brand Philosophy

Brand philosophy is quite simple, you have to determine what makes your candles/ candle making business different and perhaps better from your competitors. The candles you produce should have a certain effect on people or your target market. This is where you'll insert your own "personal touch" once you've mastered the technique in making candles, you need to make sure that your candle stands out from the rest, if you adapt a brand philosophy for your business, it'll surely drive in more sales for you.

We cannot emphasize enough how branding is an important aspect in running a candle making business, or any other business for this matter. You aren't the only one producing candles in your area for sure which is why you need to ensure that your customers will see your company/ products' edge over your competitors so that they'll keep coming back. One major tip we can give you is to first observe your competitors and see what works for them. Learn what makes them successful, and perhaps try to implement the same strategies to your own business, this way you'll speed up the process when it comes to developing your brand, marketing your products, and finding your own niche.

Decide on Your Company's Name and Logo

Once you know what kind of brand you want your company to be known for, it's time to think of a memorable company name, and logo! This is also crucial because it will serve as your customer's "recall." It has to be something that's easy to say, easy to spell, simple yet quite catchy. However, it's also important that your company name and logo follow your brand philosophy. It has to be something that when they look at it or read it, your customers will easily recognize what kind of candle company you're running. You have to start with the 'why' especially at the stage of creating a brand. You can make superb candles but if your company doesn't resonate with your customers, it wouldn't go a long way.

Think of Apple Inc., their logo is simple, the name is easy to remember, and their products are one of a kind but if you really think about it, what makes Apple really different from their competitors is their brand philosophy.

People don't buy their product because it's superb or high – tech, it's all part of that but the main reason why Apple has become one of the most successful tech companies in the world is because they adapt a very strong brand philosophy that their founder Steve Jobs had established since the very beginning – that when you buy/use their products, you are literally part of a "revolution," your part of something big, you are different. If you can embody a brand philosophy as strong as Apple, you'll be crushing your competition. People buy the company's "Why," keep that all in mind when you're thinking of a name and a logo because it will say everything about you, your business, and your products/ services.

Get Your Business Registered

Once you've figured all the important things, it's now time to get it legal! Research and do your own due diligence when it comes to registering your business. Ask mentors if you can to help you out regarding the legal side of running a business including your sales tax etc.

Establish a Selling Platform

Once your business is properly registered, you can now start thinking about ways on how to reach your future customers. It's quite easy to do that at the comfort of your own home, thanks to the internet and e – commerce websites. You can easily post your products online via Amazon.com, E-Bay.com, Shopify.com, and Etsy.com just to name a few. These online stores will allow you to easily market your products, and you'll also have access to their instant payment/ shipping systems.

It's also highly recommended that you design your own website or hire someone to do it for you. This will allow you to customize your own page, and get direct traffic as well plus in today's world, a business is usually not considered as credible if it doesn't have a website. In addition to this, you should also set up social media pages so that you can reach lots of potential customers/ big time clients. Plan your marketing strategy as this is also very important when it comes to getting the word out about your candle – making business.

Photo Credits

Page 1 Photo by user Jill111 via Pixabay.com,

https://pixabay.com/en/lights-christmas-luminaries-night-1088141/

Page 9 Photo by user Sweet Louise via Pixabay.com,

https://pixabay.com/en/candle-holders-candle-terrace-3262938/

Page 25 Photo by user Pixel 2013 via Pixabay.com,

https://pixabay.com/en/candles-church-light-lights-prayer-2628473/

Page 26 Photo by user Felix MitterMeier via Pixabay.com,

https://pixabay.com/en/candles-christmas-greeting-card-2993936/

Page 37 Photo by Homecrafts.co via Preppers.info,
http://www.preppers.info/uploads/General_-_Candle_Making.pdf

Page 39 Photo by Homecrafts.co via Preppers.info,
http://www.preppers.info/uploads/General_-_Candle_Making.pdf

Page 41 Photo by Homecrafts.co via Preppers.info, http://www.preppers.info/uploads/General_-_Candle_Making.pdf

Page 43 Photo by Homecrafts.co via Preppers.info, http://www.preppers.info/uploads/General_-_Candle_Making.pdf

Page 44 Photo by Homecrafts.co via Preppers.info, http://www.preppers.info/uploads/General_-_Candle_Making.pdf

Page 45 Photo by Homecrafts.co via Preppers.info, http://www.preppers.info/uploads/General_-_Candle_Making.pdf

Page 46 Photo by Homecrafts.co via Preppers.info, http://www.preppers.info/uploads/General_-_Candle_Making.pdf

Page 48 Photo by user Pasja 1000 via Pixabay.com,

https://pixabay.com/en/flower-tulips-love-the-ceremony-3111821/

Page 52 Photo by Homecrafts.co via Preppers.info, http://www.preppers.info/uploads/General_-_Candle_Making.pdf

Page 53 Photo by Homecrafts.co via Preppers.info, http://www.preppers.info/uploads/General_-_Candle_Making.pdf

Page 55 Photo by Homecrafts.co via Preppers.info, http://www.preppers.info/uploads/General_-_Candle_Making.pdf

Page 56 Photo by Homecrafts.co via Preppers.info, http://www.preppers.info/uploads/General_-_Candle_Making.pdf

Page 58 Photo by Homecrafts.co via Preppers.info, http://www.preppers.info/uploads/General_-_Candle_Making.pdf

Page 59 Photo by Homecrafts.co via Preppers.info, http://www.preppers.info/uploads/General_-_Candle_Making.pdf

Page 60 Photo by Homecrafts.co via Preppers.info, http://www.preppers.info/uploads/General_-_Candle_Making.pdf

Page 63 Photo by user Erika Wittlieb via Pixabay.com,

https://pixabay.com/en/candle-decorative-decoration-912773/

Page 76 Photo by user City Edv via Pixabay.com,

https://pixabay.com/en/tealight-candles-tea-lights-wax-988768/

Page 94 Photo by Nature Crafts via Gov.mb.ca, https://www.gov.mb.ca/agriculture/rural-communities/4h/pubs/candle_making.pdf

Page 96 Photo by user Jill111 via Pixabay.com,

https://pixabay.com/en/candles-valentine-valentine-s-day-2000135/

References

"Candle Making" - EduPlace.com
https://www.eduplace.com/monthlytheme/november/pdf/candles.pdf

"Candle Making" - Manitoba Department of Agriculture and the Manitoba 4-H Projects: Nature Crafts
https://www.gov.mb.ca/agriculture/rural-communities/4h/pubs/candle_making.pdf

"Candle Making" – Preppers.info
http://www.preppers.info/uploads/General_-_Candle_Making.pdf

"Candle Making – A Guide for Beginners" - SavvyHomeMade.com
https://www.savvyhomemade.com/candle-making/

"Candle Making" - CandleTech.com
https://candletech.com/candle-making/

"Candle Making" – CandlesAndSupplies.net
http://www.candlesandsupplies.net/Candle-Making

"How to Make Candles" – HobbyCraft.co.uk

http://www.hobbycraft.co.uk/supplyimages/wf1002/how-to-make-candles.pdf

"How to Make Your Own Homemade Candles" – TheSpruceCrafts.com
https://www.thesprucecrafts.com/basic-candle-making-instructions-516753

"History of Candle Making" - NaturesGardenCandles.com
https://www.naturesgardencandles.com/candlemaking-soap-supplies/item/history/-history-of-candle-making.html

"The Candle Making Manual" - NaturesGardenCandles.com
http://www.naturesgardencandles.com/mas_assets/theme/ngc/pdf/manual.pdf

"The History of Candles and Candlemaking" - CandleWic.com
https://www.candlewic.com/service/about-candlewic/the-history-of-candles-and-candlemaking/page.aspx?id=2216

Feeding Baby
Cynthia Cherry
978-1941070000

Axolotl
Lolly Brown
978-0989658430

Dysautonomia, POTS
Syndrome
Frederick Earlstein
978-0989658485

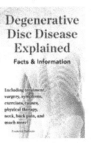

Degenerative Disc
Disease Explained
Frederick Earlstein
978-0989658485

Sinusitis, Hay Fever,
Allergic Rhinitis Explained
Frederick Earlstein
978-1941070024

Wicca
Riley Star
978-1941070130

Zombie Apocalypse
Rex Cutty
978-1941070154

Capybara
Lolly Brown
978-1941070062

Eels As Pets
Lolly Brown
978-1941070167

Scabies and Lice Explained
Frederick Earlstein
978-1941070017

Saltwater Fish As Pets
Lolly Brown
978-0989658461

Torticollis Explained
Frederick Earlstein
978-1941070055

Kennel Cough
Lolly Brown
978-0989658409

Physiotherapist, Physical
Therapist
Christopher Wright
978-0989658492

Rats, Mice, and Dormice
As Pets
Lolly Brown
978-1941070079

Wallaby and Wallaroo Care
Lolly Brown
978-1941070031

Bodybuilding Supplements
Explained
Jon Shelton
978-1941070239

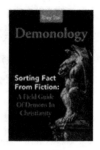

Demonology
Riley Star
978-19401070314

Pigeon Racing
Lolly Brown
978-1941070307

Dwarf Hamster
Lolly Brown
978-1941070390

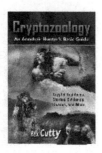

Cryptozoology
Rex Cutty
978-1941070406

Eye Strain
Frederick Earlstein
978-1941070369

Inez The Miniature Elephant
Asher Ray
978-1941070353

Vampire Apocalypse
Rex Cutty
978-1941070321